An Adult Coloring Book For Anyone With A Colorful Family

Welcome to Awkward Family Photos: The Adult Coloring Book!

The following pages have all been inspired by real awkward family photos. That's right, they're all real and they're all really awkward.

As always, we want to thank the families who have sent their photos to us - without them, none of this would be possible.

If you have a photo that you think is cringeworthy, please submit to: awkwardfamilyphotos.com/submit.

Thank you for coloring the awkwardness!

Love,
Awkward Family Photos

The Big Squeeze

WIND BENEATH MY WINGS

Look Who's Talking

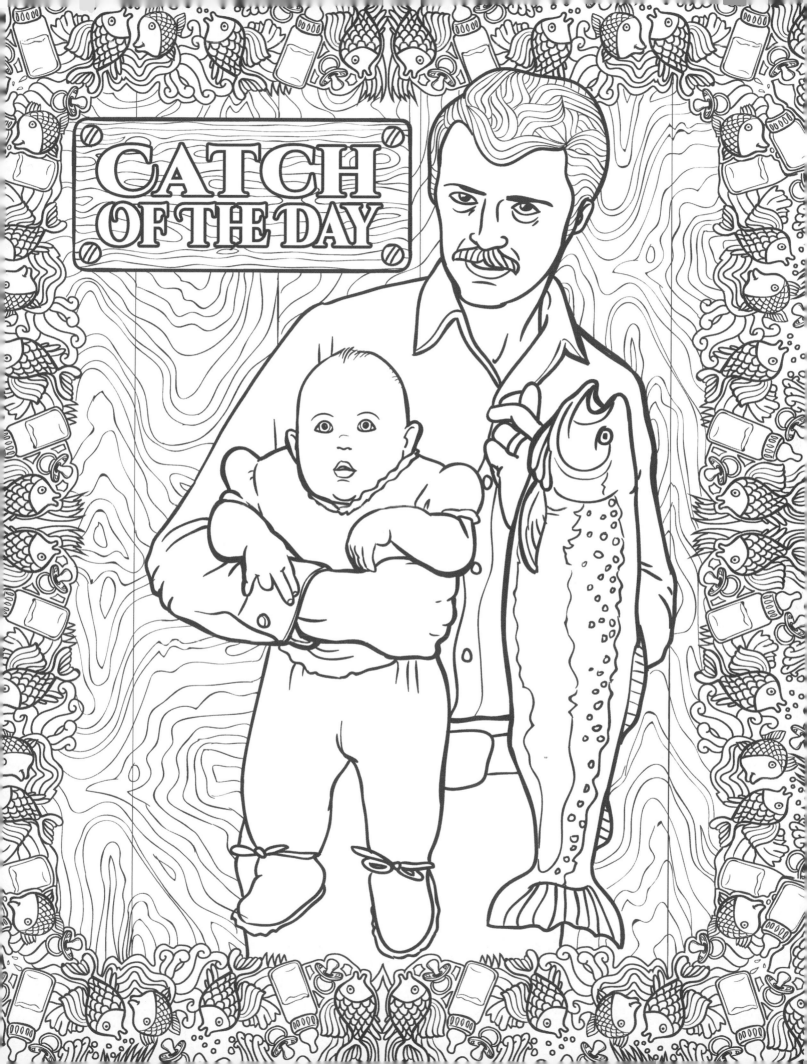

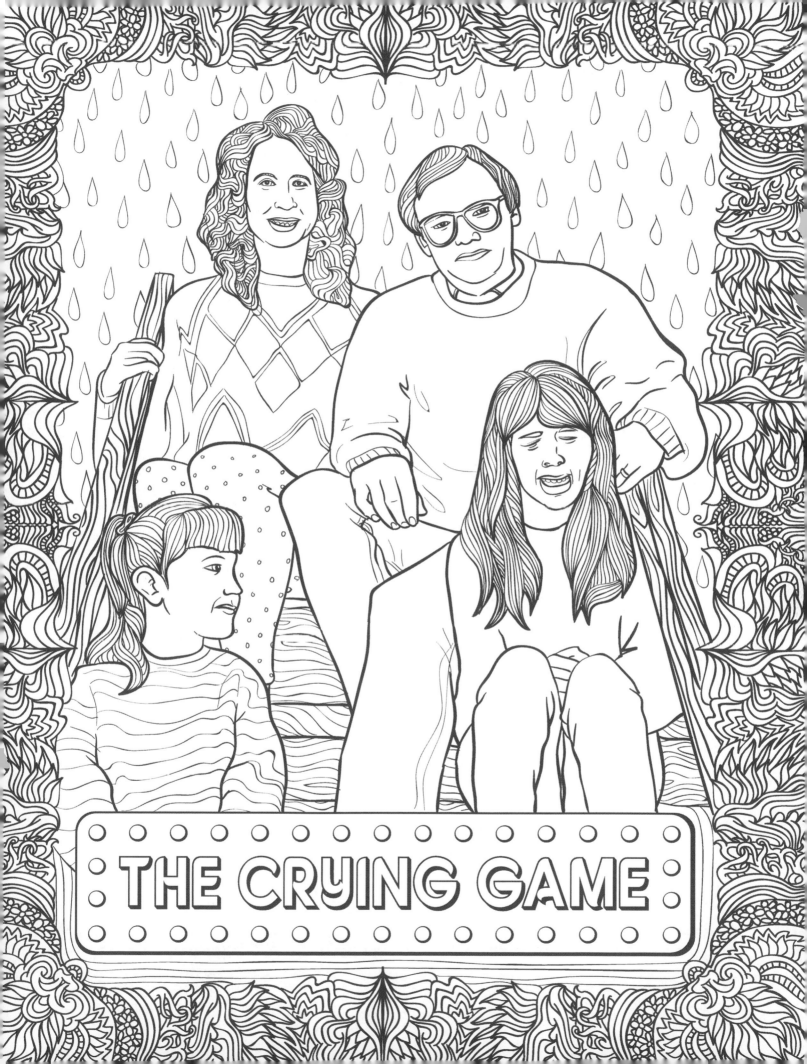

HOT CROSSED BUNS

PURE MAGIC

Simply Radishing

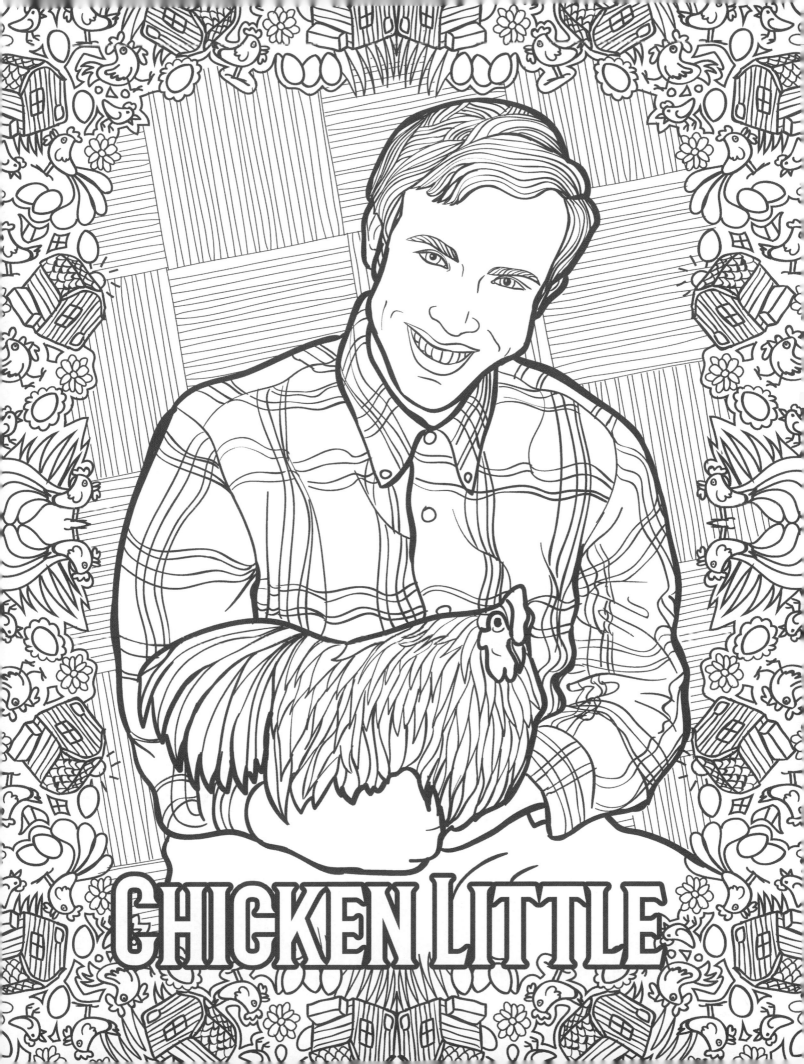

CHICKEN LITTLE

—

HEAD OF THE FAMILY

Made in the USA
San Bernardino, CA
18 November 2019